Courage to Grow

Courage to Grow
Rachel Meng

Copyright © 2025 by Rachel Meng

ISBN 979-8-89691-929-2

Courage to Grow

FROM RELATIONSHIPS TO SELF-TRANSFORMATION

Rachel Meng

Contents

Preface

As I sit on the train heading back to Ghent for the fourth time, I feel a deep sense of gratitude returning to my soul place once again. The rhythmic hum of the train prompts me to reflect on the past few years —a journey marked by both challenges and excitement. More than anything, it has been a journey of growth, often demanding courage. That courage is what inspired me to write this book. By sharing my experiences, I hope that some part of my journey resonates with you, offering guidance or comfort along the way.

Growing up, I was known as the girl with a bright smile, radiating warmth and happiness. Yet, beneath that exterior, I struggled with anxiety—a challenge that intensified during the pandemic. During that time, I turned to self-help books and sought support from therapists, both of which provided temporary relief. However, I found myself caught in a cycle, repeatedly slipping back into familiar patterns of anxiety and negative thinking. That was when I realized I needed to go beyond the surface—beyond my body and mind—to the essence of my soul.

For me, travel has always been a form of meditation in motion. Solo trips, in particular, have given me the space for deep self-reflection. Last year, I reached my 50th country, Qatar, and along the way, I have not only embraced diverse cultures but also gained profound insights. In Chapter 12 on "Mindfulness," I highlight the importance of travel and why you should never wait to embark on your own journey—for travel teaches life lessons early and deeply.

I vividly remember sitting by the canal in Leiden when I realized that happiness doesn't have to be complicated—it simply requires being present and not overthinking. In Ghent, my soul place, I learned the beauty of going with the flow and embracing life even when plans don't unfold as expected. In San Sebastián, standing atop Monte Igueldo before making my way down to the distant beach, I saw how daunting paths become manageable when taken one step at a time. In Vevey, the serenity of the lake taught me to appreciate nature and stillness. In Dubrovnik, I watched locals singing along to restaurant music and savoring their coffee for hours, reminding me to embrace life's simple joys. In Marrakesh, after thieves stole my phone, a kind local spent hours with me at the police station, demonstrating the true essence of compassion. In Budapest,

I broke my foot yet still took a night cruise on the river, letting the stunning scenery shift my focus away from pain, reinforcing the idea that mindset shapes experience. In Bogotá, when rain and fog obscured the view from Monserrate, rather than feeling disappointed, I found beauty in imperfection and saw it as a reason to return. And in Dubai, watching the Burj Al Arab against the sunset on Jumeirah Beach, I had a realization: we are only limited by our own beliefs.

While travel has played a key role in my personal growth, launching Hotel Bambinee has been another defining chapter. This urban, child-centered hotel brand was conceived in 2020, yet for five years, I faced endless challenges, doubts, and questions from others. If the idea was so promising, why hadn't a major hotel chain implemented it? Was there a reason it hadn't been done? Despite these uncertainties, I held onto my belief that the hospitality industry needed to evolve to better serve families with young children. If no one else was doing it, why couldn't I be the one to start?

Many industry professionals dismissed my vision as unrealistic, questioning why I would pursue something that wasn't guaranteed to be a financial success. But to me, hospitality is about more than profit—it's about serving people, all people, not just the most lucrative market segment. Hotel Bambinee is also committed to supporting organizations that promote children's well-being worldwide. The overwhelming support I received after launching the brand affirmed my belief in its purpose. As I discuss in Chapter 10 on "Purpose," pursuing what is meaningful to you is what truly matters. For me, that means making a difference, no matter how small, and contributing to a better world. I encourage you to follow your own passions without fear of judgment and embrace the richness of life's experiences.

In many ways, coaching mirrors this philosophy. My role as a coach is not to tell you what to do but to help you uncover what is valuable for your own transformation. That is why, in this book, I do not include personal examples from my coachees or myself—this is your journey, and only you can determine the right path.

Since I started dedicating myself to helping others as a coach, I have worked with many coachees struggling with love and relationships. Time and again, I have found that at the core of these struggles lies a lack of self-care and boundaries, often rooted in an internal sense of incompleteness. Relationships become challenging when love is sought as validation rather than as an extension of self-abundance. That realization led me to encourage my coachees to focus on their own transformation.

The book is therefore divided into two parts. The first explores key concepts in love and relationships, not just as theoretical ideas but through the lens of self-care. Many of my coachees have struggled in this area, making it difficult to cultivate healthy, fulfilling relationships. The second part focuses on self-transformation, which I believe is essential for sustaining meaningful relationships. The lessons in this section have been instrumental in my own growth, and I hope they serve as a guide for you as well.

Before closing, I want to express my deepest gratitude: to my family, whose unwavering support has shaped who I am today; to every experience—both good and bad—that has taught me invaluable lessons; and to every person who has been part of my journey, my "train ride," as I call it (see the "Train Journey Theory" in Chapter 7). Whether or not our paths cross again, I am grateful for the time we have shared, and I wish you the very best on your own journey.

Rachel Meng
Ghent, Belgium
March 12, 2025

Part
One

RELATIONSHIPS

Without trust, relationships become fragile, vulnerable to doubt, and susceptible to breakdown.

Chapter One TRUST – THE CORE OF A THRIVING RELATIONSHIP

Trust is the cornerstone of any meaningful relationship. It is the invisible thread that binds people together, fostering security, intimacy, and emotional resilience. Without trust, relationships become fragile, vulnerable to doubt, and susceptible to breakdown. Understanding the nature of trust, how to build it, and how to repair it when broken is essential to creating and sustaining strong relationships.

THE ESSENCE OF TRUST

At its core, trust is the belief in the reliability, integrity, and intentions of another person. It means feeling safe to be vulnerable, to share thoughts and emotions without fear of betrayal or judgment. Trust is cultivated over time through consistent actions, honest communication, and mutual respect. It is both a feeling and a choice, requiring conscious effort from all parties involved.

Trust is not just about believing that someone will not betray or deceive; it is also about knowing that the person will act in your best interest. Trust encompasses emotional, physical, and psychological security. In close relationships, it allows individuals to be their authentic selves without fear of criticism or rejection. It is a continuous process that requires nurturing and reinforcement.

BUILDING TRUST IN RELATIONSHIPS

Establishing trust takes time and effort. It is built through repeated interactions that reinforce reliability and emotional safety. Trust is a two-way street—both parties must contribute to its development. Here are some essential elements of building trust:

Honesty and Transparency

Honesty is the foundation of trust. Being truthful, even when the truth is difficult to share, fosters a sense of reliability. Transparency in communication, sharing thoughts, and being open about feelings and expectations prevent misunderstandings. Avoiding secrecy and deception strengthens the emotional bond and ensures both individuals feel secure.

People often fear that honesty will lead to conflict,

but avoiding difficult conversations can do more harm than good. Authentic relationships thrive on open dialogue, even when the truth is uncomfortable. It is important to communicate openly about needs, fears, and concerns.

Consistency in Actions

Trust is built through repeated positive interactions. When actions align with words, it creates a sense of security. Being dependable, keeping promises, and showing up when needed reinforce trustworthiness. Inconsistent behavior, on the other hand, can erode trust over time.

Consistency is especially important in relationships where trust has been previously damaged. Small, reliable actions over time can rebuild confidence and demonstrate commitment. Predictability in behavior helps individuals feel safe and valued.

Vulnerability and Empathy

Being open and vulnerable invites trust. When individuals share their fears, aspirations, and insecurities, they create deeper connections. Equally important is empathy—the ability to understand and validate another's emotions, demonstrating care and concern. When someone feels heard and understood, it strengthens their belief in the relationship.

Vulnerability is often mistaken for weakness, but

in reality, it is one of the strongest demonstrations of trust. When people allow themselves to be seen and accepted for who they truly are, they create a strong foundation for intimacy and connection. Empathy, in turn, fosters an environment where vulnerability is met with compassion rather than judgment.

Respect for Boundaries

Respecting each other's boundaries—whether emotional, physical, or psychological—signals consideration and integrity. It reassures individuals that their needs and comfort levels will be honored. Boundaries help create a sense of personal security, ensuring that neither person feels overwhelmed or disrespected.

Boundaries are unique to each relationship and must be communicated clearly. For instance, some people need personal space, while others require frequent emotional reassurance. Honoring these preferences fosters mutual respect and strengthens trust.

Effective Communication

Clear, honest, and respectful communication reduces misunderstandings and fosters trust. Active listening, acknowledging concerns, and expressing feelings constructively are vital aspects of maintaining an open dialogue. Miscommunication and assumptions can quickly erode trust, making it essential to clarify intentions and actively engage in discussions.

Communication is not just about speaking; it is also about listening. Active listening involves being fully present, avoiding interruptions, and responding thoughtfully. When individuals feel heard, they are more likely to trust their partners and open up about their own experiences.

Mutual Support and Reliability

Trust is reinforced when individuals demonstrate unwavering support for each other in times of crisis or need. Being present, offering encouragement, and standing by each other through life's challenges cement a strong foundation of trust.

A reliable partner is one who not only makes promises but also follows through on them. Small gestures, such as remembering important dates or checking in regularly, show dependability and genuine investment in the relationship's well-being.

WHEN TRUST IS BROKEN

Trust, once broken, can be challenging to rebuild. However, it is not impossible. Acknowledging the breach, taking responsibility, and making amends are critical first steps. Genuine remorse, coupled with consistent efforts to restore faith, can slowly heal wounds.

Betrayal can take many forms, from lies and broken promises to emotional or physical infidelity. Regardless of the nature of the breach, the steps to rebuilding trust remain the same:

Steps to Rebuilding Trust:

- **Acknowledge the hurt:** Recognizing the pain caused and validating the affected person's emotions is essential. Dismissing or minimizing the hurt only deepens the wound.
- **Take responsibility:** Owning up to mistakes without justifying or blaming helps in regaining credibility. An apology should be sincere and free of excuses.
- **Make amends:** Genuine efforts, such as changed behavior and reassurance, demonstrate a commitment to repairing the relationship. This may include setting new boundaries or making compromises to rebuild security.
- **Be patient:** Trust is not rebuilt overnight. It takes time, effort, and a series of positive experiences to restore confidence. Both parties must be willing to work through the pain and commit to the process.

Rebuilding trust is a gradual process that requires transparency, forgiveness, and renewed commitment. While some relationships recover stronger than before, others may not survive a severe breach of trust. In such cases, it is important to recognize when it is time to walk away and prioritize personal well-being.

WHEN DISHONESTY BECOMES A CHRONIC ISSUE

When lies enter the equation, they chip away at that foundation of trust. While a single lie might seem small, habitual dishonesty creates deep cracks that are difficult to mend. The deceived partner may struggle with lingering doubt, questioning every word and action. This constant state of unease is emotionally exhausting and can damage one's well-being.

Address dishonesty with open communication. When dishonesty arises, approaching the situation with open and honest communication is the key. Instead of reacting with anger or accusations, try to understand why the lie was told. Some people lie out of fear, insecurity, or a desire to avoid conflict. By maintaining a calm mindset, both partners can work toward a resolution.

Enforce your boundaries. Boundaries define acceptable behavior and reinforce self-respect. If a partner consistently lies, they are disregarding those boundaries and the emotional impact of their actions.

Enforcing boundaries communicates self-worth and ensures that your needs are met. Remember, you receive what you tolerate —so set clear boundaries that protect your well-being. Respect yourself enough to walk away from situations that diminish your peace, confidence, or happiness.

Prioritize self-care. Lying is a form of emotional manipulation that distorts reality and creates an unhealthy power dynamic. Constantly questioning a partner's words and actions can lead to anxiety, self-doubt, and emotional exhaustion. When the stress of dishonesty overshadows the joy and security of the relationship, it's time to prioritize self-care.

Trust your instincts. If something feels off, do not ignore it. Gaslighting and deception can make you question your own perceptions, but your feelings are valid. A relationship should uplift you, not leave you in a constant state of doubt and distress. If your partner is unwilling to be truthful and respect the trust you have given them, the healthiest choice may be to walk away.

* * *

A relationship built on trust flourishes. It fosters emotional safety, deepens intimacy, and creates a solid foundation for growth. Trust enables partners to navigate conflicts constructively, support each other through life's challenges, and experience a profound sense of connection.

When trust is present, relationships feel lighter and more fulfilling. There is less fear, doubt, and insecurity. Instead, there is a deep sense of confidence in each other's loyalty and support. Trust allows individuals to take risks, knowing they have someone to rely on. Moreover, relationships built on trust are more likely to withstand external pressures, whether financial hardships, family conflicts, or personal struggles. The ability to rely on one another provides a sense of stability and hope.

While mistakes can happen and trust can sometimes be rebuilt, habitual lying signals a fundamental lack of respect. Setting boundaries, addressing dishonesty, and prioritizing self-care are crucial steps in protecting yourself and maintaining a relationship grounded in honesty and mutual respect. At the end of the day, a relationship should bring joy, security, and respect. Never settle for less than you deserve.

Self-Care Tips for Building and Maintaining Trust:

- **Be honest and transparent:** Share your thoughts and emotions openly, even when the truth is difficult. Honest communication fosters trust and reduces misunderstandings.
- **Embrace vulnerability and empathy:** Share your insecurities and feelings, and practice empathy toward

your partner. This strengthens emotional intimacy and deepens the connection.

- **Practice effective communication**: Engage in active listening and express feelings constructively. Avoid assumptions to prevent misunderstandings that can erode trust.
- **Address dishonesty openly:** When dishonesty arises, approach the situation calmly and communicate openly. Understand the reasons behind the dishonesty, but enforce your boundaries firmly.
- **Prioritize self-care:** If dishonesty becomes chronic, it can emotionally drain you. Trust your instincts and prioritize self-care to protect your mental and emotional well-being.
- **Know when to walk away:** If a relationship continues to undermine your trust and well-being despite efforts to resolve issues, prioritize your own health and happiness by considering walking away.

Without communication, relationships become unsustainable, as unmet needs and unspoken expectations create distance and frustration.

Chapter Two

COMUNICATION – THE KEY TO BUILDING LASTING LOVE BEYOND FANTASY

In any relationship, communication is the foundation upon which trust, understanding, and connection are built. However, it is easy to get lost in the fantasy of love—the idealized version of what we want a relationship to be—rather than focusing on the reality of what it requires. True love isn't just about feelings or dreams; it is about being open, honest, and clear with each other. Without communication, relationships become unsustainable, as unmet needs and unspoken expectations create distance and frustration. To build a lasting, fulfilling partnership, it is essential to move beyond fantasy and embrace the challenging yet rewarding work of clear, honest communication.

STOP FANTASIZING: IS YOUR ATTRACTION BASED ON REALITY OR ILLUSION?

Love is often romanticized in movies, books, and even in our own minds. We may create an idealized version of a partner before we truly get to know them, filling in the blanks with our desires and expectations. But when the reality of who they are does not match our fantasy, disappointment sets in.

Ask yourself: Are you in love with who this person truly is, or with an image you have constructed? Pay attention to what is left unsaid in your relationship. Are there stories that have not been shared? Are you only seeing the best side of your partner while ignoring red flags? A healthy relationship is built on a real connection, not just projections of who we want the other person to be.

Infatuation is a great example of falling for an idealized version of someone. During the infatuation phase, we tend to focus on their "perfect" qualities, often overlooking deeper issues or incompatibilities. This intense attraction can feel exciting, but it is based on a fantasy rather than the reality of who the person truly is. True love requires seeing your partner as they are, flaws and all, and building a connection grounded in authenticity and mutual understanding.

HOW TO BREAK FREE FROM FANTASY

Observe, don't assume. It is easy to project our own expectations and ideals onto a partner, but true understanding comes from paying close attention to their values, habits, and behaviors. Instead of assuming who they are or what they believe, take the time to observe how they interact with others, handle challenges, and express their emotions. This approach helps build a realistic perspective rather than an illusion based on personal desires.

Ask meaningful questions. Instead of relying on assumptions, engage in discussions that reveal your partner's true personality, beliefs, and aspirations. Open-ended questions about their past experiences, goals, and values can provide valuable insight into who they really are. When you take the time to truly listen, you gain a clearer picture of their authenticity rather than the version you may have imagined.

Pay attention to inconsistencies. If someone repeatedly makes promises but fails to follow through, or if their behavior contradicts their words, do not ignore these red flags. Discrepancies between what a person says and what they do often reveal deeper truths about their reliability and character. Facing these inconsistencies with awareness prevents you from falling deeper into a fantasy that may not align with reality.

Give the relationship time to unfold naturally. Strong relationships develop over time through shared experiences, challenges, and trust. Moving too quickly risks investing in a fantasy rather than the actual person in front of you. Give yourself the space to see the relationship for what it truly is, allowing emotional intimacy to develop at a healthy pace.

By embracing these principles, you create a foundation for relationships based on truth, connection, and genuine compatibility rather than illusion.

COMMUNICATE YOUR DEAL BREAKERS IN ADVANCE

One of the most crucial aspects of a successful relationship is setting clear expectations. Many couples avoid difficult conversations early on, fearing they will drive the other person away. However, unspoken deal breakers can lead to resentment and conflict down the line.

If something is non-negotiable for you—whether it is honesty, loyalty, financial responsibility, or family values—communicate it openly. Some people believe that small lies or white lies are harmless, while others see them as a breach of trust. If honesty is essential for you, say it outright.

When communicating your deal breakers, **be upfront while maintaining kindness**. Setting boundaries does not mean being confrontational;

rather, it allows you to express your needs in a way that fosters understanding and respect. By approaching the conversation with a calm and open mindset, you can ensure that your message is received without causing unnecessary conflict.

Using clear and direct language is essential. Instead of vague statements like, "I don't like dishonesty," be specific: "If I find out you've lied to me, even about something small, it will break my trust." This level of clarity leaves no room for misunderstanding and helps set clear expectations from the start.

Encourage an open discussion by allowing your partner to express their own non-negotiables. This fosters mutual understanding and ensures that both individuals are on the same page. This dialogue allows for a more balanced and fair approach to setting relationship expectations.

Lastly, **do not compromise on your core values** to keep the peace. Suppressing your needs may lead to resentment or dissatisfaction in the long run. Staying true to your values ensures that your relationship aligns with what you genuinely want and need for long-term happiness.

COMMUNICATE WHAT'S IMPORTANT TO YOU AND SET BOUNDARIES

A relationship without clear communication is like a ship without a compass. If you do not express what matters to you, how can your partner know how to meet your needs?

Boundaries are not about controlling the other person; they define what you will and will not accept. They provide clarity and prevent misunderstandings, ensuring that both partners feel respected and valued.

Identify your priorities—what makes you feel valued, respected, and safe? Effectively communicating your needs and boundaries in a relationship starts with self-awareness. Understanding what behaviors or actions are unacceptable to you is just as important as knowing what you need from a partner. By defining these aspects for yourself first, you will be better equipped to express them clearly to others.

Use "I" statements. Instead of saying, "You never make time for me," which sounds accusatory, try, "I feel loved when we spend quality time together. Can we prioritize that?" This approach keeps the conversation constructive and fosters collaboration rather than defensiveness. By focusing on your feelings and desires rather than placing blame, you create a more open and understanding dialogue.

Reinforce your boundaries when necessary. Tolerating toxic behavior can be detrimental to your emotional well-being. If your partner exhibits unhealthy behaviors, confront them as soon as they occur. Ignoring red flags or postponing difficult conversations leads to resentment and worsens issues over time. If something in your relationship bothers you, address it promptly. Open and honest communication is key to preventing small concerns from turning into major conflicts. A simple, firm reminder can prevent misunderstandings and reinforce that your boundaries deserve to be respected and emphasize your self-worth.

Active listening and open-mindedness foster a relationship built on mutual respect and support. Communication is a two-way street. Just as you want to be heard and understood, your partner should feel comfortable expressing their needs as well. Creating a space where both individuals can communicate freely, you strengthen your connection and ensure that both partners feel valued.

LET GO OF THE FANTASY OF CHANGE

Many people hold onto the hope that their partner will eventually confess to their wrongdoings and change their behavior. While it is natural to want to believe in the best version of someone, it is important to recognize when this hope becomes a trap. Waiting for an untrustworthy partner to admit fault and transform can keep you stuck in a cycle of disappointment and emotional pain.

Let go of the fantasy and embrace reality. If a person repeatedly crosses your boundaries and refuses to take responsibility, their actions speak louder than words. Change is only possible if someone acknowledges their mistakes and actively works to correct them. If they continue to dismiss your concerns, it is unlikely they will suddenly have a moment of realization and become the partner you wish them to be.

COMMUNICATION MISTAKES TO AVOID

Effective communication is essential for a healthy relationship. Nevertheless, certain communication mistakes can harm your connection with your partner:

- **Do not repeatedly bring up past mistakes.** While it is important to discuss past issues affecting your present relationship, continuously revisiting them will only cause further distress.
- **Avoid labeling or criticizing your partner's personality.** Focus on how their actions make you feel instead of using hurtful labels. For example, rather than saying, "You're a liar," express, "I felt hurt when I discovered that what you said wasn't true." This approach fosters constructive dialogue rather than conflict.
- **Acknowledge mistakes and apologize when necessary.** Everyone makes mistakes; recognizing them and apologizing sincerely fosters growth and understanding.

* * *

Love without communication is unsustainable. It's easy to fall in love with an idea, but lasting relationships require honesty, clarity, and openness. By stepping away from fantasy, discussing deal breakers early, and clearly communicating your needs and boundaries, you create a foundation for a fulfilling and authentic partnership. The right person won't be afraid of these conversations—they'll welcome them, knowing that open communication is the key to a successful relationship.

Self-Care Tips for Breaking Free from Fantasy in Relationships:

- **Stop fantasizing:** See your partner for who they truly are, flaws and all, rather than an image you've created.
- **Observe, don't assume:** Instead of making assumptions about your partner, pay attention to their actions, values, and behaviors. This helps you understand them realistically.
- **Ask meaningful questions:** Engage in deep, open-ended conversations to gain deeper understanding about your partner's true personality, beliefs, and experiences.

- **Pay attention to inconsistencies:** If your partner's words don't align with their actions, address the discrepancies to avoid getting caught in an illusion.
- **Give the relationship time to develop:** Allow the relationship to evolve at a natural pace, giving emotional intimacy time to grow before jumping into deep commitments.
- **Communicate deal breakers early:** Be upfront about your non-negotiables (e.g., honesty, loyalty, values) to avoid misunderstandings later on.
- **Set clear boundaries:** Define what is acceptable and what isn't in the relationship. Express needs and limits with clarity, using "I" statements to avoid blame.
- **Avoid the fantasy of change**: Don't hold onto the hope that a partner will change on their own. If someone continually disrespects your boundaries, it is unlikely they will change without sincere effort.
- **Avoid communication pitfalls**: Avoid repeatedly bringing up past mistakes, labeling your partner negatively, or focusing on personality traits. Instead, focus on how their actions make you feel.

When we love
unconditionally, we do not
seek validation, rewards,
or guarantees. Instead we
choose to give love freely,
simply for the joy of
sharing it.

Chapter Three

UNCONDITIONAL LOVE – THE POWER OF LOVING UNCONDITIONALLY

Unconditional love is often considered as the purest form of love—one that exists without conditions, expectations, or the need for reciprocation. It originates from a place of self-abundance rather than longing or deficiency. When we love unconditionally, we do not seek validation, rewards, or guarantees. Instead we choose to give love freely, simply for the joy of sharing it.

THE CHARACTERISTICS OF UNCONDITIONAL LOVE

Emotional Security and Stability

One of the greatest gifts of unconditional love is the emotional safety it provides. When partners know they are loved without conditions, they feel secure in the relationship. This security allows them to be vulnerable, express their true feelings, and navigate challenges without fear of abandonment.

Forgiveness and Understanding

Mistakes are inevitable in any relationship. Unconditional love makes room for forgiveness and understanding rather than holding grudges or resorting to punishment. It prioritizes resolving conflicts with empathy rather than blame.

Support Through Life's Challenges

Unconditional love does not waver when life becomes difficult. Whether facing financial struggles, health issues, or emotional setbacks, partners who practice unconditional love stand by each other, offering comfort, reassurance, and strength.

Loving Without Fear

Conditional love often breeds anxiety and insecurity, as people feel they must constantly prove their worth or meet expectations to remain loved. Unconditional love eliminates this fear, offering reassurance that love is not based on achievements or external factors but on a genuine, heartfelt connection.

Love Without Expectations

Many relationships operate on the principle of transactional love, where affection is given with an expectation of something in return. Unconditional love, however, thrives in the joy of giving and caring without keeping score. This does not mean tolerating mistreatment or neglect, but rather, loving from a place of emotional abundance rather than need.

LOVE FROM A PLACE OF SELF-ABUNDANCE

The ability to love unconditionally begins with cultivating a deep sense of self-love. This means:

- **Knowing your worth:** When you truly recognize your value, you no longer depend on others for validation or approval. Your self-esteem should be rooted in your own understanding of who you are, rather than being shaped by external opinions. This inner confidence allows you to engage in relationships as an equal partner, rather than seeking love to compensate for a lack of self-worth.
- **Having emotional independence:** True love is about complementing, not completing, one another. Emotional independence means not placing the

weight of your happiness on your partner. Love should not be a demand for constant devotion, but rather a balance between togetherness and personal fulfillment. Expecting your partner to dedicate all their time and energy to you is not only unrealistic but also unhealthy. Rather than relying on your partner to fulfill all your emotional needs, cultivate self-confidence and fulfillment in different areas of your life. Engage in hobbies that bring you joy, spend quality time with loved ones, and invest in your personal growth. By doing so, you create a sense of completeness within yourself rather than seeking it solely from your relationship. You take responsibility for your own emotional well-being while still sharing love, support, and companionship with your significant other. This balance creates a relationship based on mutual respect rather than dependence.

- **Practicing self-care:** Taking care of yourself emotionally, mentally, and physically ensures that you are in the best position to offer love without conditions. By prioritizing your well-being, you bring a healthier, more fulfilled version of yourself into your relationships. This, in turn, enables you to love with greater compassion, patience, and understanding.

- **Letting go of control:** True love allows space for individuality and growth. When you love yourself fully, you no longer feel the need to control your partner; you accept and appreciate them for who they are, creating a relationship built on trust and genuine connection.

Love that comes from self-abundance is effortless and sustainable. It does not drain or deplete but rather enriches both individuals in the relationship.

NURTURING UNCONDITIONAL LOVE IN A ROMANTIC RELATIONSHIP

Unconditional love is not something that simply exists; it must be cultivated through daily actions, mindset shifts, and intentional efforts.

Practice Acceptance

True love begins with accepting your partner for who they are, rather than who you want them to be. This means appreciating their strengths while also embracing their flaws. It is important to support personal growth without forcing change upon them.

Communicate Openly and Honestly

Unconditional love thrives on honest and open communication. Expressing feelings, needs, and concerns with transparency creates trust and understanding. Active listening and empathy also play crucial roles in fostering emotional connection.

Let Go of Unrealistic Expectations

Many relationships suffer because partners hold on to unrealistic expectations of one another. While shared goals and values are important, demanding perfection can lead to disappointment. Instead, focus on appreciating the love and effort your partner brings to the relationship.

Prioritize Emotional and Physical Presence

Being present for your partner—both emotionally and physically—reinforces love and connection. Whether through meaningful conversations, shared experiences, or simple gestures of affection, presence is a powerful way to show unconditional love.

Develop a Deep Sense of Empathy

Empathy is the ability to understand and share your partner's emotions. Practicing empathy means putting yourself in their shoes, validating their feelings, and offering support without judgment. It strengthens the bond between partners and creates a nurturing environment for love to grow.

Offer Love Freely Without Keeping Score

In relationships where love is conditional, partners may feel pressured to reciprocate affection in equal measure. However, in unconditional love, acts of kindness and affection are given freely, without expecting anything in return.

Support Your Partner's Growth

A healthy relationship fosters personal growth. Unconditional love encourages dreams, provides reassurance during setbacks and supports a partner's evolution into their best self.

Forgive and Let Go of Resentment

Holding onto grudges creates emotional barriers in a relationship. Practicing forgiveness allows partners to move forward with love and understanding. While it is important to set healthy boundaries, choosing love over resentment leads to a deeper emotional connection.

Maintain Boundaries and Independence

It is essential to maintain individuality and continuing growing outside the relationship. Pursue personal passions, maintain friendships, and invest in personal development. Encouraging each other's independence strengthens trust and respect within the relationship.

UNCONDITIONAL LOVE VS. ACCEPTING TOXIC BEHAVIOR

Loving unconditionally does not mean tolerating mistreatment, disrespect, or neglect. True love must be built on mutual respect and care. Staying in an abusive relationship under the guise of 'unconditional love' can be harmful. Love should uplift, not diminish, and accepting mistreatment can lead to a loss of self-worth and emotional exhaustion.

If a partner continuously disregards your well-being, breaks trust, or engages in toxic behaviors, unconditional love should not be an excuse to stay in a harmful relationship. Instead, self-love should guide you to walk away from situations that compromise your dignity and emotional health.

*　*　*

Unconditional love is not about losing yourself in a relationship or ignoring your own needs. It is about choosing to love from a place of strength and generosity. When we stop seeking love to complete us and instead offering love as a gift, relationships flourish in profound and lasting ways.

The power of unconditional love lies in its ability to create a bond based on true acceptance, patience, and unwavering support—an unshakable foundation for any meaningful relationship.

Self-Care Tips for Loving Unconditionally:

- **Self-love is key:** Recognize your worth and cultivate emotional independence to reduce the need for external validation.
- **Emotional independence**: Find personal fulfillment outside of the relationship to avoid excessive dependence on your partner for happiness.
- **Prioritize self-care**: Taking care of your emotional, mental, and physical well-being allows you to love freely and without conditions.
- **Maintain boundaries**: Protect your individuality by setting healthy boundaries and avoiding emotional entanglement.
- **Let go of control**: Accept your partner's individuality and allow space for growth without trying to change them.
- **Avoid toxic behavior**: Unconditional love does not mean tolerating

mistreatment; set boundaries and walk
away from relationships that compromise
your well-being.

True compassion uplifts and nurtures both partners and serves as a bridge that allows them to grow together while maintaining their individual well-being.

Chapter Four

COMPASSION – A BALANCED APPROACH TO LOVE AND CARE

Compassion in a romantic relationship is the ability to empathize with your partner's emotions and respond with care and understanding. It is an active choice to be present, supportive, and loving, even in difficult times. Unlike fleeting acts of kindness, compassion is a deep-seated commitment to your partner's well-being.

Nevertheless, compassion must be balanced. It should never lead to self-sacrifice or enable unhealthy behaviors. True compassion uplifts and nurtures both partners and serves as a bridge that allows them to grow together while maintaining their individual well-being.

THE KEY COMPONENTS OF COMPASSION IN LOVE

Emotional Understanding

At the heart of compassion is the ability to recognize and validate your partner's emotions. This involves active listening, genuine empathy, and a willingness to understand their feelings without immediately offering solutions or dismissing concerns.

A compassionate partner takes the time to ask, "How are you feeling?" and truly listens to the response. They acknowledge their partner's emotions, whether it is joy, sadness, frustration, or fear, and offer comfort and reassurance instead of judgment or dismissal.

Patience and Forgiveness

No relationship is without its challenges, and misunderstandings are inevitable. Compassion allows couples to approach conflicts with patience rather than frustration. Instead of reacting impulsively, a compassionate partner seeks to understand the root of an issue before responding.

Forgiveness is another crucial aspect of compassion. Holding onto resentment creates emotional distance, while choosing to forgive and move forward strengthens the relationship. Compassionate partners do not dwell on past mistakes but rather use them as opportunities to grow together.

Acts of Kindness and Thoughtfulness

Small, everyday acts of kindness reinforce compassion in a relationship. Whether it is making your partner's favorite meal, leaving a thoughtful note, or offering a comforting hug, these gestures show that you care. Kindness is the glue that holds relationships together, reminding partners that they are loved and appreciated.

Thoughtfulness also extends to understanding your partner's needs and acting accordingly. A compassionate partner anticipates their loved one's struggles and offers support before being asked. These small moments of consideration create a strong foundation of trust and emotional security.

Being Present in Moments of Pain

Compassion is most needed during times of struggle. When a partner is going through a difficult time —whether due to work stress, personal loss, or mental health challenges—a compassionate partner offers a safe space to process emotions.

Being present doesn't necessarily mean fixing the problem. Sometimes, all that is needed is a listening ear, a warm embrace, or the reassurance that they are not alone. The simple act of showing up in moments of pain is one of the most powerful expressions of love.

Unconditional Support and Encouragement

Compassionate relationships thrive when both partners feel encouraged to pursue their dreams and overcome obstacles. Encouragement is a form of love that instills confidence and security. It reassures partners that they have someone in their corner, cheering them on through life's challenges.

Supporting your partner's aspirations, being their biggest cheerleader, and believing in their potential fosters a deep sense of emotional security. A compassionate partner celebrates victories, no matter how small, and provides reassurance during setbacks.

COMPASSION WITHOUT SELF-SACRIFICE

Compassion and forgiveness are essential in a relationship; nonetheless, do not confuse them with tolerating mistreatment. Being kind does not mean allowing someone to disrespect, manipulate, or hurt you. Only you can decide what you will and won't tolerate—no one else can make that choice for you. If you allow repeated mistreatment, it is essential to reflect on why you are accepting that behavior and what steps you need to take to protect yourself.

Establishing clear boundaries is non-negotiable.

Boundaries are not walls to shut people out; they are guidelines that define what is acceptable and what isn't. They protect your emotional and mental health and ensure that your compassion isn't exploited. Remember, you teach others how to treat you by the standards you set and enforce.

Many people believe that sacrificing themselves in a relationship is noble—that giving everything to another person is an act of love. But love does not require you to deplete yourself. There is nothing honorable about losing your own well-being for the sake of someone else's happiness. If you consistently put others' needs ahead of your own, you will eventually experience burnout, resentment, and emotional exhaustion. You deserve a relationship where love is reciprocal, where your energy is replenished rather than drained.

COMPASSION DOESN'T MEAN YOU'RE MEANT TO BE TOGETHER

Feeling deeply for someone's pain also does not mean you are meant to be with them romantically. It's easy to mistake emotional connection for something more profound, especially when you feel drawn to someone who is struggling. But keep in mind: you are looking for a partner, not a patient.

For example, if your partner has Narcissistic Personality Disorder, no matter how much compassion you have for them, you have to be careful about entering into a relationship with them. Narcissists often struggle with empathy, manipulate others to meet their needs, and create a dynamic where you are constantly giving while they are taking. Your compassion will not change them; instead, you may find yourself drained—emotionally, mentally, and even physically. Recognizing this distinction is crucial because no amount of love or understanding can replace the personal accountability they need to take for their own healing.

A healthy relationship thrives on mutual emotional support, not on one person constantly carrying the weight of the other. If you find yourself repeatedly drawn to those who need "fixing," ask yourself why. Is it a pattern? Do you believe your love can heal someone else's wounds? While love is power-ful, it is not a replacement for personal healing, nor should it be.

EVERYONE MUST WALK THEIR OWN HEALING JOURNEY

Healing is a personal journey—one that no one else can walk for them. You can be a source of kindness and encouragement, but you cannot force someone to heal, nor can you take on their suffering as your own. When you do, you risk losing yourself in their strug-gles, making their problems your problems. And in the end, you cannot live someone else's life for them.

In Buddhism and Dharma teachings, this concept

is beautifully expressed as the balance between compassion and wisdom. Compassion urges us to care and empathize with others, but wisdom reminds us to stay grounded in the reality that healing is an internal process. Maintaining this balance allows you to be present for others while safeguarding your own well-being.

A compassionate partner understands the difference between supporting and rescuing. Support means standing by someone as they do the work themselves. Rescuing means doing the work for them, which is neither sustainable nor healthy.

* * *

Compassion is one of the most vital components of a healthy and thriving romantic relationship. It fosters understanding, emotional intimacy, and resilience, allowing couples to navigate challenges with kindness and grace. A relationship rooted in compassion is one in which both partners feel valued, supported, and deeply connected.

However, being compassionate does not mean losing yourself in someone else's struggles. Love should not be about fixing or saving; it should be about growing together as equals. Respect your partner's healing journey, establish healthy boundaries, and remember that a truly loving relationship should nurture both individuals.

Self-Care Tips for Practicing Compassion:

- **Balance compassion with wisdom:** Care for others while staying grounded in reality. A healthy relationship replenishes your energy rather than draining it. Prioritize mutual support over self-sacrifice.
- **Support, don't rescue:** You can encourage a partner's healing, but you cannot take on their struggles. Everyone must walk their own healing journey.
- **Set clear boundaries**: Compassion does not mean tolerating mistreatment. Define what is acceptable and enforce standards that protect your well-being.
- **Recognize when compassion becomes a trap**: Feeling for someone's pain does not mean you are meant to be with them. Be mindful of relationships where you give endlessly while receiving little in return.

You deserve a relationship that aligns with your values, brings you joy, and allows you to be your best self. If that isn't what you have now, it may be time to let go.

Chapter Five

WHEN TO LET GO OF A RELATIONSHIP

Romantic relationships are complex, dynamic, and often unpredictable. They begin with excitement, passion, and the promise of shared dreams, but over time, circumstances, personal growth, and evolving desires can introduce challenges. At some point in many relationships, the question arises: "Should we stay, or should we let go?"

Letting go of a relationship is never easy. It requires courage, introspection, and sometimes painful realizations. However, staying in a relationship that no longer serves you can be just as damaging as leaving one prematurely. This chapter explores when it might be time to let go of a romantic relationship and how to navigate that decision with compassion and clarity.

KEY SIGNS AND CONSIDERATIONS

Misalignment in Values and Goals

One of the most telling signs that a relationship may not have a future is a fundamental misalignment in values and long-term goals. Where do you see yourself in the future? Does your partner share a similar vision? If, for example, one of you strongly desires marriage and monogamy while the other prefers a more open or independent lifestyle, this discrepancy can cause ongoing tension and resentment. There is no right or wrong answer—only what aligns with your authentic self. Consider whether your present joy is enough, or if a shared future is key to your happiness.

The Best Friend Test

Imagine your best friend going through the same struggles you are facing in your relationship. What advice would you give them? If you would encourage them to walk away, why should your own situation be any different? Often, we are kinder and more objective when offering guidance to others, but applying that same wisdom to ourselves can bring much-needed clarity.

The Regret Test

Another powerful tool is to imagine yourself many years down the road, reflecting on this relationship. Will you regret ending it, or will you regret staying? Be honest with yourself. If you foresee consequences that make staying feel like a source of future regret, that may be your gut or instinct telling you it is time to walk away. Conversely, if the thought of ending it brings lasting doubt and sorrow, that's worth exploring further before making a decision.

When You No Longer Recognize Yourself

A relationship should bring out the best in you. If you start disliking the version of yourself that emerges in the relationship—whether due to emotional distress, insecurity, or unhealthy behavioral patterns—it may be a sign that the relationship is no longer serving your well-being. Your happiness, confidence, and self-respect should never be compromised. **Never lose yourself trying to fit into someone else's expectations. The right relationship will embrace you as you are, encouraging growth without requiring you to sacrifice your authenticity.**

When Pain Outweighs Joy

One of the most obvious signs that a relationship might need to end is persistent unhappiness. **Life is too short to be spent in a relationship that brings more pain than joy.** While every relationship has its ups and downs, a pattern of chronic dissatisfaction can signal a deeper issue that cannot be resolved by mere effort or time.

- **Emotional exhaustion**: You feel drained emotionally after spending time with your partner, and the emotional effort required to maintain the relationship feels heavier than the emotional reward it provides.
- **Constant conflict**: You and your partner are constantly arguing, and even after discussions, the same issues resurface without resolution. Communication breaks down, and there is no longer a sense of mutual understanding or respect.

Knowing Your Deal Breakers

Every individual has personal deal breakers—non-negotiable boundaries that define the integrity of a relationship. These may include trust, honesty, communication, and respect. If trust has been repeatedly broken, whether through dishonesty, betrayal, or other forms of disrespect, the relationship can become toxic.

- **Infidelity**: While some relationships can survive infidelity with open communication and mutual effort, for many, it signifies an irreversible breach of trust. If attempts to rebuild trust have failed, letting go may be the most honorable decision.
- **Lies and Secrets**: If one or both partners are hiding things or regularly lying, the relationship begins to lose its integrity. Even small lies, when compounded, can create a feeling of emotional distance that is hard to overcome.

If a relationship consistently violates your core values, it is time to reevaluate whether it is worth continuing. You deserve a relationship built on mutual love, respect, and emotional security. **Never settle for less than what aligns with your worth and well-being.**

Unwillingness to Resolve Issues

No relationship is without its struggles. However, what truly matters is whether both partners are willing to acknowledge issues and work toward resolution. If your partner actively participates in problem-solving and shows genuine commitment to growing with you, then the relationship may be worth saving. But if they deny problems, refuse accountability, or dismiss your feelings, it may be a sign that things will never improve.

One of the biggest mistakes people make in relationships is assuming that their partner will change. While growth and improvement are possible, you cannot force someone to become someone they are not. Rather than hoping they'll change, consider: Can you accept them as they are? If the answer is no, it may be time to walk away.

Abuse or Manipulation

This is one of the most serious and clear-cut signs that a relationship should end. Abuse, whether physical, emotional, or psychological, is never acceptable. No one should remain in an abusive relationship, regardless of the circumstances.

- **Physical Abuse**: Any form of physical harm, no matter how minor it may seem, is a red flag.
- **Emotional and Psychological Abuse**: Manipulation, belittling, or controlling behaviors create a toxic environment that undermines your mental and emotional health.

- **Gaslighting**: A partner who constantly questions your perceptions or manipulates situations to make you feel crazy or insecure is engaging in gaslighting. This is a destructive form of emotional abuse.

Feeling Unsupported

In a healthy relationship, both partners should feel supported emotionally, mentally, and physically. A lack of support in a relationship can manifest in various ways:

- **Emotional neglect**: One partner may be emotionally distant, unavailable, or uninterested in the other's feelings, creating a one-sided dynamic where one person is constantly giving and the other is constantly taking.
- **Absence of encouragement**: If your partner does not celebrate your successes, acknowledge your struggles, or support your personal growth, it can leave you feeling undervalued and isolated.

Trusting Your Gut

Your intuition is powerful. If you have repeatedly felt uneasy, doubtful, or sensed red flags throughout the relationship, don't ignore those feelings. Your gut instinct is often the first indicator that something is not right. Trust yourself enough to walk away when your inner voice tells you it's time.

The Right Time Is Now

If a breakup seems inevitable, delaying it only prolongs the pain. Many people stay in relationships out of fear of being alone or hoping that things will improve. or simply because they are accustomed to their partner's presence. But deep down, if you know that a breakup is the healthiest option, then there is no better time than now to take that step.

ENDING ON A BEAUTIFUL NOTE

Sometimes, relationships end not because they were bad, but because they have served their purpose. People come into our lives for a reason—some to teach us, some to grow with us, and some to show us a love that, while not meant to last forever, was still meaningful. Choosing to part ways when there are still good memories allows both partners to walk away with gratitude rather than bitterness. It is better to end on a high note than to wait until love turns into resentment.

Parting with beautiful memories means carrying forward the lessons learned, the laughter shared, and the moments that made your heart full. **Instead of focusing on the loss, focus on the growth and**

the joy that the relationship brought into your life. The end of one chapter does not erase the beauty of the story that was written; it simply paves the way for a new beginning.

A graceful goodbye is a testament to the love and respect that once existed. It allows both individuals to move forward with peace, knowing that their time together was not wasted but instead a meaningful part of their journey. When a relationship ends in love rather than in pain, it leaves both souls free to embrace what the future holds with an open heart.

* * *

Letting go of a relationship can be one of the most difficult yet liberating decisions you ever make. It requires self-awareness, courage, and the willingness to prioritize your well-being. Remember, choosing to leave a relationship that no longer serves you is not a failure—it is an act of self-love. You deserve a relationship that aligns with your values, brings you joy, and allows you to be your best self. If that isn't what you have now, it may be time to let go.

Self-Care Tips for Knowing When to Let Go of a Relationship:

- **Assess value alignment:** If your core values and long-term goals don't align with your partner's, the relationship may not have a sustainable future.

- **Use the Best Friend and Regret Tests:** Ask yourself what advice you'd give a friend in your situation and whether you'll regret staying or leaving in the long run.

- **Stay true to yourself:** A healthy relationship should uplift you, not make you feel lost or insecure. Never shrink yourself to fit into someone else's expectations.

- **Weigh pain vs. joy:** If a relationship brings more emotional exhaustion, unresolved conflict, or unhappiness than joy, it may be time to move on.

- **Know your deal breakers**: Trust, honesty, respect, and communication are non-negotiable. If these are repeatedly broken, reconsider the relationship's future.

- **Don't stay hoping they'll change:** Love cannot force someone to grow. Accept your partner as they are or recognize when change is not likely to happen.

- **Recognize abuse and manipulation:** Any form of physical, emotional, or psychological abuse is a clear sign to leave.

Trust your instincts and prioritize your safety.

- **Seek emotional support and encouragement:** A partner should uplift and support your growth. If you feel emotionally neglected or undervalued, the relationship may be unhealthy.
- **Trust your intuition:** If something feels consistently wrong, listen to your gut. It often senses problems before your mind fully acknowledges them.
- **Let go with grace:** Not all relationships are meant to last forever. Ending things with love and gratitude allows both partners to move forward with peace and new possibilities.

True growth happens when we let go of what no longer serves us, creating room for new opportunities and relationships that align with who we are now.

Chapter Six GROWING BEYOND HEARTBREAK

Breakups often feel like the closing of a chapter—a painful goodbye to what once felt like an integral part of our lives. However, if we shift our perspective, past relationships can be seen not as failures but as mirrors reflecting the parts of ourselves that still need healing and growth. Every relationship we enter is an opportunity for self-discovery—an invitation to better understand our desires, patterns, and wounds. This chapter explores how we can grow beyond heartbreak, transforming pain into a catalyst for a healthier and more fulfilling future.

RECOGNIZING THE PATTERNS

Have you ever found yourself repeatedly drawn to the same type of partner? Perhaps they share similar traits—emotionally unavailable, overly dependent, or even manipulative. If so, it is not a coincidence; it is a pattern. The root of this attraction often lies within us. Are we overcompensating for low self-esteem? Do we nurture others excessively because we lack boundaries? Are we seeking validation from our partners due to deep-seated insecurities?

A breakup provides a crucial moment for reflection. **Ask yourself: "What am I missing within myself that I keep searching for in others?"** By answering this question, you begin the process of healing. You start to realize that your worth isn't determined by a partner's love or approval but by your own self-acceptance and growth.

EMBRACING GROWTH AND HEALING FROM PAST TRAUMA

Moving on from a past relationship doesn't mean erasing its existence. Instead, it means transforming pain into wisdom and allowing ourselves the space to heal. Our ability to find joy and fulfillment lies within our control. The present is a gift, and by embracing the opportunities each new day brings, we step into a future of self-empowerment and inner peace.

Healing is not a linear journey—it comes with ups and downs, moments of strength, and moments of vulnerability. It requires patience and self-compassion. Grieving the loss of a relationship is natural and necessary. Cry if you need to, write your feelings in a journal, or talk to a trusted friend or therapist. Acknowledging your emotions helps to release them, making room for growth.

Self-care is an essential part of this healing process. Engage in activities that nourish your mind and soul—exercise, meditation, creative pursuits, or spending time in nature. Rediscover hobbies and passions that may have been neglected during the relationship. Each act of self-care reinforces your independence and reminds you that your happiness is not tied to another person.

One of the most difficult parts of healing after heartbreak is the process of forgiveness. Whether it is forgiving your ex for their actions, forgiving yourself for any mistakes you feel you made, or even forgiving the circumstances that led to the end of the relationship, forgiveness is a powerful tool for healing.

Forgiveness is not about condoning the behavior that caused you pain, nor is it about letting the person who hurt you off the hook. Rather, it is about freeing yourself from the emotional grip of anger, resentment, and hurt. Holding onto grudges only keeps you tethered to the past and prevents you from moving forward.

Furthermore, it is important to **reframe your thoughts about the breakup.** Instead of seeing it as a failure, view it as an experience that taught you valuable lessons about love, boundaries, and self-worth. Growth comes from reflection, and by recognizing what worked and what did not, you are better equipped for future relationships. The end of one love story is not the end of your capacity to love—it is simply a redirection toward something more aligned with your true self.

When nostalgia creeps in, remind yourself: missing someone does not mean you need them back in your life. It simply means they played a role in your journey, and that role has reached its conclusion. Cherish the good times, but don't let them anchor you to the past.

CHOOSING GROWTH OVER REGRESSION

Choosing growth over regression means allowing yourself to move forward, even when it feels difficult. It's about recognizing that healing requires space and that holding onto someone from your past can prevent you from embracing what lies ahead. While it may be tempting to maintain a connection for comfort or nostalgia, true growth happens when we let go of what no longer serves us, creating room for new opportunities and relationships that align with who we are now.

If you are considering reconnecting with a former partner, take a moment to reflect: Why do you want to reconnect? Is it because you truly believe in the possibility of growth together, or is it driven by loneliness, fear of change, or nostalgia for what once was?

Many people also wonder whether maintaining a friendship with an ex is possible or advisable. More often than not, remaining friends creates confusion, reopens emotional wounds, and hinders the ability to move forward. Emotional attachments take time to dissolve, and forcing a friendship can prolong the healing process.

There is a reason why an ex is called an "ex." Always remember why you made that decision in the first place. The deal-breakers that led to the breakup have not magically disappeared, and revisiting the past will not change what was not meant to be. Instead, focus on the future. Your happiness should not depend on someone else's presence in your life. **The love you seek begins with the love you cultivate for yourself.**

Your ex is also on their own journey of growth. They, too, need space to heal, reflect, and evolve. Closure is an act of self-care, and sometimes, the best way to honor a relationship is to leave it in the past.

FOR THE BELIEVERS OF TWIN FLAMES AND SOULMATES

If you believe in soulmates or twin flames, remember that these concepts should never trap you in a relationship that no longer serves you. The right person will never require you to stay in a place of suffering.

Breaking up does not mean losing a soulmate—it means that if you are truly meant to be, the universe will find a way to bring you back together once you have both healed and evolved. If not, then the connection was a lesson, not a destiny.

FINDING BEAUTY IN IMPERFECTION

If you find yourself deeply grieving the end of a relationship, allow it. There is beauty in incompleteness. Have you ever wondered why heartbreaking love stories resonate so deeply? It is because they reflect the imperfection of life—and that imperfection is what makes life meaningful. **Learn to appreciate all emotions and simply let them pass.**

Emotions, like all experiences, are fleeting. While it is natural to feel pain, sadness, or loss, remember that these emotions are not permanent. They are part of the human experience and offer valuable insights into who we are and how we navigate the world. When we allow ourselves to fully feel, without resistance, we create space for healing and growth. In this way, the beauty of imperfection becomes a source of strength, resilience, and deeper understanding.

Be grateful for the love you experienced, even if it did not last forever. Many people go through life without ever feeling such deep emotions. Your pain is proof that you lived, that you loved, and that your heart is capable of profound connection. Be grateful for the person you were in love with, and even though the relationship had to end, continue to wish them the very best—from your heart and from afar. Replace resentment with compassion and gratitude, for these emotions will allow you to heal faster and bring you peace as you move forward.

THE POWER OF LETTING GO

True healing begins when we acknowledge that clinging to the past prevents us from embracing the future we deserve. **Releasing someone is an act of self-respect and self-love.** When we let go, we free ourselves from the chains of the past and welcome new opportunities, people, and experiences into our lives. The past is not where your happiness lies.

Letting go does not mean suppressing emotions. It means fully processing them—feeling the sadness, anger, and confusion—then deciding to move forward. It requires learning to trust the journey and having faith that what lies ahead is far greater than what is left behind.

When we find ourselves looking back, reminiscing, and questioning whether we made the right decision, remind yourself of why you walked away. Recall the lessons learned, the moments of clarity, and the reasons you knew you had to move on. Letting go is not a one-time act but a continuous choice to prioritize your well-being and future happiness. Take stock of all the present possibilities and appreciate all that you have in the present. Focus on cultivating your own happiness and abundance.

* * *

Each breakup is an invitation to grow, to reflect, and to heal. The pain you feel now is temporary, but the wisdom you gain from this experience will last a lifetime. When you look back, you'll realize this chapter was never about loss—it was about becoming the person you were always meant to be.

Self-Care Tips for Healing from Heartbreak:

- **Reflect on patterns**: Identify recurring relationship habits and recognize what you seek in others that you may need to cultivate within yourself.
- **Prioritize healing:** Allow yourself to grieve, process emotions, and engage in self-care activities.
- **Practice forgiveness**: Let go of resentment toward yourself or your ex to free yourself from emotional weight.
- **Choose growth over regression:** Avoid revisiting the past or reconnecting with your ex; trust that letting go creates space for better opportunities.
- **Reframe the breakup**: See it as a lesson and opportunity to focus on self-

love and personal growth rather than failure.

- **Embrace letting go:** Accept that closure comes from within and that true happiness lies in your present and future, not in the past.

Part

Two

SELF-TRANSFORMATION

Love and compassion begin within. By cultivating self-love, embracing your unique journey, and showing gratitude for every person who crosses your path, you create a life of deeper meaning and purpose.

Chapter Seven LOVE AND COMPASSION

Love and compassion are foundational elements of the human experience. They shape the way we connect with others, guide our personal growth, and transform the world around us. While these virtues are often discussed in relation to how we treat others, they are equally important in how we treat ourselves. The foundation of a meaningful and purposeful life is built on self-love and acceptance—embracing our unique journeys and the lessons they bring. Love isn't something we seek; it's something we nurture within ourselves. As we do, it radiates outward, touching everyone we encounter. By being kind to ourselves, honoring our own paths, and allowing love to guide us, we create a life filled with connection, purpose, and profound compassion.

THE IMPORTANCE OF SELF-LOVE

The most important relationship you will ever have is the one with yourself. Loving yourself is not selfish; it is a necessity. Self-love is often misunderstood as selfishness, but the two concepts are vastly different. **Self-love is not about prioritizing your own needs at the expense of others, nor is it about ego or arrogance. Rather, it is about honoring your own needs, boundaries, and well-being while also extending that same kindness and care to others.** When we practice self-love, we not only take care of ourselves but also set an example for others on how to love and care for themselves.

Prioritizing yourself is an act of self-respect and self-care—one that should never be postponed. The investment you make in yourself—physically, mentally, emotionally, and spiritually—shapes every aspect of your life. If you have been waiting for the "perfect" moment to start working out, take that class you have always dreamed of, or chase that passion that sets your soul on fire, stop waiting. The right time is now. Your dreams and goals deserve immediate attention. When you take care of yourself, you show up as the best version of yourself in your relationships and contributions to the world. Self-love fuels confidence, inner peace, and a deeper sense of fulfillment.

Incorporate this question into your daily routine: **"How can I enhance my well-being?"** Your well-being should never be an afterthought. Prioritizing what nurtures your happiness, soothes your soul, and strengthens your spirit is the foundation of a fulfilling life.

ACCEPTANCE – EMBRACING WHO YOU ARE AND WHO YOU ARE NOT

True self-love comes with full acceptance— not only of who you are but also of who you are not. There is immense freedom in acknowledging both your strengths and limitations. You do not have to fit into anyone else's mold or chase an unrealistic ideal. You are enough as you are. This acceptance is not about complacency but about understanding yourself deeply and loving yourself unconditionally.

Embrace your uniqueness, honor your values, and let go of the need for external validation. When you accept yourself wholly, you liberate yourself from unnecessary comparisons and societal pressures, allowing space for authentic growth and happiness. Never question yourself or your decisions—trust that you made the best choice given the circumstances at the time. Self-doubt only holds you back, while self-acceptance empowers you to move forward with confidence and peace.

COMPASSION FOR YOURSELF AND OTHERS WHILE HOLDING FIRM BOUNDARIES

Compassion is the ability to empathize with the suffering of others and take action to alleviate it. It involves recognizing that pain is a shared human experience and extending kindness, care, and understanding to those who are struggling. Compassion is not just about offering sympathy; it's about actively supporting others on their journey to healing. When we show empathy toward others, we create a space for healing, trust, and mutual respect. Everyone carries unseen burdens, and a little kindness can make a profound difference in someone's life. Understanding others' perspectives strengthens relationships, resolves conflicts, and builds a more supportive and harmonious world.

Showing compassion to others reflects a kind heart, but it does not mean allowing people to overstep your boundaries. True compassion does not require enduring toxicity or sacrificing your well-being. Real love includes the ability to say "no" when necessary, stand firm in your truth, and protect your energy from those who drain it. True compassion is about balance—it allows us to uplift others while also honoring our own needs. **It is possible to be both firm and kind, to set boundaries while still offering love, and to be understanding without compromising our well-being.** By practicing both compassion and self-respect, we create healthier, more fulfilling relationships and a stronger sense of inner peace.

Equally important is practicing compassion towards ourselves. Many people are quick to show kindness to others but struggle to extend that same compassion to themselves. We often hold ourselves to higher standards than we hold others, and when we make mistakes or fall short, we are quick to criticize ourselves. **To practice self-compassion, we must recognize that we deserve the same care and understanding we offer to others.**

CHOOSING LOVE OVER FEAR

Every decision we make is either rooted in love or in fear. When faced with a choice, ask yourself: Am I doing this out of love, or am I doing it out of fear? Love fosters courage, kindness, and authenticity, while fear breeds insecurity, doubt, and avoidance.

Fear-based decisions often lead to regret, as they stem from a place of lack and hesitation. Love-based decisions, on the other hand, lead to growth, connection, and fulfillment. Whether it's pursuing a dream, expressing your true feelings, or making a life-changing choice, **let love be your guiding force**—love for yourself, love for others, and love for the journey itself.

THE TRAIN JOURNEY THEORY

Life is a journey, much like a train ride. Each of us is on our own path, moving toward unique destinations. Along the way, we share parts of our ride with fellow passengers—friends, family, partners, and acquaintances. Some stay for a long time; others only for a brief moment. Some bring us joy, laughter, and deep connection, while others challenge us, teach us difficult lessons, or even cause us pain. Yet, no matter their role, each person is part of our journey for a reason.

It is important to appreciate every person who crosses your journey, regardless of whether they bring joy or hardship. Every interaction carries a lesson, an opportunity for growth, or a moment of connection. However, just as we have our own journey, so do they. It is selfish to ask someone to stay when it is their time to move on. Likewise, we should never abandon our own train ride to board someone else's, no matter how much we want to be with them. Our path is ours alone, and deviating from it for the sake of another risks losing our true selves.

Cherish those who travel alongside you, enjoy their presence while they are there, and bid them farewell with love and gratitude when their time comes to step off. Wishing them well on their journey reflects love and understanding—a testament to the beauty of shared experiences without attachment.

THE RIPPLE EFFECT OF LOVE AND COMPASSION

Love and compassion are contagious. When we practice these virtues, they ripple outward, affecting those around us and fostering a culture of kindness and understanding. Acts of love, whether big or small, inspire others to do the same. A kind word or a simple gesture can brighten someone's day and set off a chain reaction of positivity.

The more we cultivate love and compassion in our own lives, the more we contribute to a collective sense of well-being. Our actions, words, and attitudes have the power to create a world that is more caring, empathetic, and connected.

* * *

Love and compassion begin within. By cultivating self-love, embracing your unique journey, and showing gratitude for every person who crosses your path, you create a life of deeper meaning and purpose. Be kind to yourself, honor your journey, and let love lead the way. The more you nurture love within, the more it radiates outward, touching everyone you encounter on this beautiful train ride called life.

In a world that often feels divided and disconnected, love and compassion offer a pathway to healing and unity. They remind us that we are all in this together and that by caring for ourselves and others, we can create a more harmonious and peaceful world.

Self-Care Tips for Nurturing Love and Compassion:

- **Practice self-love**: Prioritize your well-being by honoring your needs and boundaries. Self-love is the foundation of confidence, fulfillment, and meaningful relationships.
- **Embrace acceptance:** Love yourself as you are, acknowledging both your strengths and limitations. Let go of societal pressures and self-doubt.
- **Set healthy boundaries:** Show compassion to others without sacrificing your own needs.
- **Extend compassion to yourself:** Be as kind to yourself as you are to others.
- **Choose love over fear**: Base your decisions on love and courage rather than fear and doubt.
- **Appreciate the journey:** Recognize that everyone you meet has a role in your

life's journey. Cherish lessons and
connections, and let go when it's time.

- **Create a ripple effect:** Spread love and
compassion through simple actions,
knowing that these positive energies will
inspire others and contribute to a more
caring world.

Courage is the willingness to step into the unknown with faith in oneself, even when doubt whispers loudly.

Chapter Eight COURAGE

Courage is the backbone of transformation, the fuel of pioneers, and the hallmark of those who dare to dream beyond limitations. It compels us to step beyond the familiar, challenge the status quo, and embrace the unknown with conviction.

Courage is often misunderstood as the absence of fear. Many believe that courageous individuals are those who never feel afraid. In reality, courage exists precisely because fear is present. Without fear, there would be no need for courage.

Fear is a natural human emotion that arises when we face the unknown or perceive a threat. It can hold us back from pursuing our dreams, taking risks, and making meaningful changes in our lives. Courage, then, is not about eliminating fear but about choosing to act regardless. It is the decision to move forward even when the outcome is uncertain, failure is possible, or the stakes feel high. It is the willingness to step into the unknown with faith in oneself, even when doubt whispers loudly.

By leaning into our fears, embracing discomfort, and staying committed to our goals, we build a reservoir of strength that helps us face future challenges with greater confidence.

HOW TO CULTIVATE COURAGE

While courage may seem like an innate trait, it is also a skill that can be developed over time. Like a muscle, the more we exercise courage, the stronger it becomes. Here are some strategies to help nurture and cultivate it:

- **Start small**: Courage does not always require grand, dramatic actions. Sometimes, it is about taking small steps outside your comfort zone. Speaking up in a meeting, trying a new activity, or having a difficult conversation can all build confidence and resilience.
- **Embrace imperfection**: Perfectionism can be a barrier to courage. The fear of making mistakes or failing may prevent us from attempting new things. Accept that imperfection is a natural part of growth and learning.

- **Shift your mindset**: A fixed mindset—believing that abilities are static—can prevent risk-taking. A growth mindset, on the other hand, encourages viewing challenges as opportunities for learning and development.

- **Visualize success**: Fear often arises from focusing on what could go wrong. Instead, shift your attention to what could go right by visualizing success. Imagine yourself overcoming obstacles and thriving in spite of adversity.

- **Surround yourself with support**: Build a support system of people who uplift you and believe in your potential.

- **Act despite fear**: The most important step in cultivating courage is to take action. Waiting for fear to disappear before taking action only prolongs the process. Take one step at a time and trust in your ability to navigate challenges.

BE THE PIONEER: INITIATE CHANGE

History is written by those who dare to defy norms, challenge the comfortable, and push the boundaries of possibility. The world has never been changed by those who waited for permission—it has been shaped by individuals with the audacity to initiate change, disrupt the norm, and present new ideas with unwavering belief.

Consider the pioneers of the past—people like the Wright brothers, who dared to believe humans could fly, or the tech visionaries who redefined communication. They faced skepticism, doubt, and resistance, yet they persevered. Why? Because they had the courage to stand firm in their convictions.

If you feel called to create something new, be the pioneer. The world needs trailblazers who are unafraid to disrupt the familiar and build the extraordinary.

PIVOT AND PURSUE WHAT MATTERS

Life is not a linear journey, and courage is essential when making the difficult but necessary decision to pivot. It takes boldness to acknowledge that a path once chosen is no longer the right one. Walking away from comfort to pursue what truly ignites your soul requires immense bravery.

Many people wait—wait for the perfect moment, wait for fear to subside, or wait for validation. But waiting is the enemy of progress. **If you feel drawn toward a different path, pursue it now.** Change is daunting, but stagnation is far worse. Whether it is changing careers, moving to a new place, or following a long-held dream, courage is the key to unlocking a life of fulfillment. The moment you take the first step, you set in motion the transformation that leads to your truest self.

At the same time, let go of the outcome and embrace the journey. Too often, we fixate on where we are headed and forget to appreciate the present moment. True fulfillment comes not just from achieving a goal but from the experiences, lessons, and growth along the way.

Life is meant to be explored, not controlled. Pivot boldly, pursue what excites you, and trust that every step—regardless of where it leads—will shape you into who you are meant to become. The joy is in the journey, not just the destination.

THE COURAGE TO BE YOURSELF

Authenticity is an act of bravery in a world that often pressures individuals to conform. To be yourself—unapologetically and fully—is one of the greatest displays of courage. Vulnerability is not a weakness; it is a testament to your strength and willingness to be seen, and your openness to connect with others on a profound level.

When you show up as your true self, you inspire others to do the same. Your passion, honesty, and authenticity can ignite change in others. By embracing who you are and letting your true self shine, you create a ripple effect—encouraging others to shed their masks and live more freely.

STEP BEYOND COMFORT AND EMBRACE THE LIMITLESS

The comfort zone is a silent trap—it feels safe but ultimately stifles growth. Courage is what pushes you beyond that boundary, testing your limits and proving you are capable of far more than you imagined. Growth and self-discovery happen where discomfort meets determination.

You are limitless. The only restrictions that exist are those you impose upon yourself. Why accept limitations when you have the ability to transcend them? Do not fear your own potential—your greatness is not something to be afraid of but to embrace. **Every challenge, every fear, every hesitation is an opportunity to prove to yourself that you are stronger than you think.** The world does not benefit from you playing small. Take risks, embrace discomfort, and step fully into your power.

* * *

Courage is the foundation of a life well-lived. It empowers you to be a pioneer, pivot toward your true calling, embrace authenticity, and push beyond self-imposed limitations. Do not wait for the right moment. Do not hesitate in the face of doubt. Act now, step forward with bravery, and create a life driven by boldness, adventure, and the relentless pursuit of your dreams.

Self-Care Tips for Cultivating Courage:

- **Start small:** Build courage by taking small, manageable steps outside your comfort zone. Each small action boosts your confidence and resilience.
- **Embrace imperfection**: Let go of perfectionism. View mistakes as growth opportunities.
- **Shift your mindset:** Adopt a growth mindset and believe that failure is a stepping stone, not a setback.
- **Visualize success**: Combat fear by focusing on potential success. Visualize yourself overcoming obstacles and achieving your goals to strengthen your courage.
- **Surround yourself with support:** Build a network of people who uplift and encourage you. Their support will bolster your courage and confidence.
- **Act despite fear**: Courage isn't about waiting for fear to disappear; it's about taking action anyway. Trust in your ability to handle challenges as they arise.
- **Be the pioneer**: Challenge norms and dare to create change. Be bold enough to initiate ideas and pursue what others might deem impossible.

- **Pivot boldly:** When something isn't working, have the courage to change course. Embrace new opportunities and pursue what truly excites you.
- **Be authentic**: Show up as your true self. Vulnerability is a strength, and embracing your authenticity will inspire others to do the same.
- **Step beyond comfort:** Push past the comfort zone to uncover your limitless potential.

Be thankful for the challenges that have helped you grow, for the abundance that surrounds you right now, and for the radiant energy that flows from your heart when you live in gratitude.

Chapter Nine GRATITUDE

Gratitude is often regarded as a simple concept: appreciating what you have and saying thank you for the good things in your life. However, true gratitude goes beyond mere politeness or acknowledgment—it is an active force, a mindset that can transform your life. When you approach life with gratitude, you shift your energy and perspective in profound ways.

THE SCIENCE BEHIND GRATITUDE

Recent studies in psychology have shown that gratitude has measurable physical and emotional benefits. Neuroscientific research has demonstrated that expressing gratitude triggers the release of neurotransmitters such as dopamine and serotonin, which are linked to feelings of happiness and well-being.

This means that gratitude not only brings immediate joy but also has lasting effects on overall mood.

A study conducted by Dr. Robert Emmons, one of the leading researchers on gratitude, found that people who practiced gratitude regularly reported higher levels of happiness and fewer symptoms of depression. Participants who kept a gratitude journal for just a few weeks showed significant improvements in their well-being, with many experiencing a stronger sense of optimism and deeper connections with others.

Furthermore, gratitude has been linked to improved physical health. Research suggests that people who practice gratitude are more likely to engage in healthy behaviors, such as exercising regularly, eating well, and getting enough sleep. The positive emotional effects of gratitude can also enhance immune function, lower blood pressure, and increase longevity.

GRATITUDE FOR BOTH THE GOOD AND BAD EXPERIENCES

Many of us are quick to feel gratitude for joyful and successful moments. We are thankful for good health, loving relationships, financial stability, and personal achievements. These blessings are easy to recognize and appreciate.

But what happens when life takes a turn for the worse? When challenges arise, we often feel defeated, frustrated, or angry, making gratitude the last thing on our minds. Yet, this is where true transformation lies. Even difficult, painful, and challenging experiences hold the potential to teach us something invaluable.

Every setback, hardship, or moment of discomfort offers an opportunity for growth. When you cultivate gratitude for all experiences—not just the easy ones—you acknowledge the value in every moment. These challenges shape your character, provide valuable lessons, and sometimes lead to breakthroughs that set you on a new path.

Think about a time in your life when you faced a challenge that, in hindsight, became a turning point. Perhaps a difficult job change pushed you toward a more fulfilling career, or a relationship loss helped you discover your own strength and resilience. Though painful at the time, these moments ultimately became catalysts for growth.

By shifting your mindset to one of gratitude, you begin to see the lessons hidden in every experience. You can thank life for teaching you resilience, patience, courage, and wisdom. In this way, difficulties transform from burdens into blessings, no longer weighing you down but instead lifting you up.

GRATEFUL FOR ABUNDANCE IN THE PRESENT MOMENT

It is easy to look ahead, dreaming of the things we want or believe we need to feel fulfilled. We chase the next goal, the next milestone, the next success. Yet, true abundance is not something that exists only in the future—it is available to us right now. Recognizing and appreciating the abundance in the present moment is essential.

Abundance is not just about wealth or material possessions; it includes your health, relationships, talents, and opportunities. When you pause to take stock of your life, you may realize how much you truly have. **The simple, everyday blessings we often overlook are a form of abundance.** Your ability to breathe, the love of friends and family, the freedom to make choices—these are all gifts.

Take a moment to reflect on what you have in this very moment. Be grateful for the simple things. Perhaps you have food to eat, a roof over your head, or the energy to get through your day. Maybe you have the ability to choose how you spend your time or the health to enjoy activities that bring you joy. Recognizing the abundance in the present moment helps you embrace gratitude fully and understand that everything you need is already here.

CHANGE YOUR NARRATIVE AND LET GRATITUDE RADIATE

Gratitude is not just a passive feeling; it is an active force that shapes your reality. The stories we tell ourselves create our experiences. If you view life through the lens of scarcity or lack, you will continue to see more of it. However, when you shift your narrative to one of abundance, possibility, and gratitude, you begin to notice more blessings, opportunities, and positive experiences flowing into your life.

You have the power to rewrite your story. It all comes down to changing how you frame your experiences. Instead of seeing obstacles, view them as opportunities to grow. Instead of focusing on what is missing, focus on what is present and what is possible.

When you let gratitude radiate from within, you invite positive energy into your life. Gratitude is contagious. By expressing gratitude through words, actions, or simply embodying a positive attitude, you inspire others to do the same. This creates a cycle of positivity, uplifting and empowering everyone involved.

This energy attracts more of the same. When you practice gratitude, you naturally draw more things to be grateful for. The universe responds to your vibration. Like the law of attraction, what you focus on expands. If you focus on gratitude, your life will fill with more blessings.

MAKING GRATITUDE A HABIT

Like any other practice, gratitude requires intentionality and consistency. It is easy to forget to be thankful when caught up in the busyness of life. Nevertheless, by incorporating small, mindful practices into your daily routine, you can make gratitude a habit.

Here are several practical ways to cultivate gratitude:

- **Keep a gratitude journal:** One of the most effective ways to practice gratitude is to keep a daily journal. Write down three things you are grateful for each day. These can be big or small, personal or external. The key is to focus on the positive and acknowledge it.
- **Express gratitude verbally:** Make a habit of telling others what you appreciate about them. Whether it is a family member, friend, colleague, or even a stranger, expressing gratitude can brighten their day and deepen your connection.
- **Practice mindful gratitude:** In moments of stress or frustration, take a few deep breaths and pause to reflect on what you are grateful for. This practice helps you center yourself and shift your focus away from negativity.

- **Create gratitude rituals:** Incorporate moments of gratitude into your daily routine. This could be as simple as pausing before a meal to give thanks for the food or taking a moment in the morning to reflect on what you are grateful for.

* * *

When you choose gratitude, you choose a life full of possibilities. You embrace a life that reflects your highest potential and invites more joy, love, and abundance into your experience. It is time to change your narrative, embrace the power of gratitude, and let it guide you toward the life you deserve.

So today, take a moment to reflect on all that you have, all that you have experienced, and all the opportunities before you. Be thankful for the challenges that have helped you grow, for the abundance that surrounds you right now, and for the radiant energy that flows from your heart when you live in gratitude.

Self-Care Tips for Cultivating Gratitude:

- **Embrace gratitude for all experiences**: Be grateful not only for the good times but also for challenges, as they offer growth and lessons.

- **Recognize present abundance**: Focus on the blessings you have right now, such as health, relationships, and everyday joys.
- **Shift your narrative**: Change how you view your life—focus on abundance and possibility instead of scarcity and lack.
- **Make gratitude a habit**: Practice gratitude daily by keeping a journal, expressing thanks to others, and incorporating mindful moments of appreciation into your routine.

True purpose is about fulfillment—about engaging with the world in a way that resonates deeply with who we are at the most fundamental level.

Chapter Ten PURPOSE

Purpose is the compass that guides us toward a meaningful and fulfilling life. It is the driving force that propels us forward, giving direction to our aspirations and depth to our existence. Discovering your true calling is not about waiting for a grand revelation; it is about looking inward, reflecting on your experiences, and recognizing the patterns that define you.

Life has a deeper meaning than merely achieving goals or attaining success. While external accomplishments can bring satisfaction, they are often fleeting. True purpose is about fulfillment—about engaging with the world in a way that resonates deeply with who we are at the most fundamental level.

Purpose can take many forms. It might be about the work we do, the relationships we cultivate, the creative expressions we pursue, or the impact we seek to have on the world. Regardless of its specific, purpose is the force that gives our actions meaning and provides us with a sense of belonging, fulfillment, and peace.

DISCOVERING YOUR PURPOSE

Your purpose lies at the intersection of three key elements:

- **What you spend the most time on**: Pay attention to how you naturally allocate your time. What activities engage you so deeply that hours pass without notice? Often, the things we do effortlessly hold clues to what we are meant to pursue.
- **What you are most passionate about**: Passion ignites purpose. Consider the topics, causes, or creative pursuits that excite you—the things you could discuss endlessly without boredom. Your purpose is often intertwined with what brings you joy and meaning.
- **What you have struggled with the most**: Life's challenges are not just obstacles; they are teachers that shape perspective and resilience. The difficulties you have faced may hold the key to how you can serve others, offering guidance, empathy, and wisdom.

When you find alignment in these three areas, you begin to uncover your deeper calling.

ASK YOURSELF: WHAT MATTERS MOST?

The first step in finding purpose is gaining a deeper understanding of ourselves. Self-awareness involves exploring who we are, what we value, and what motivates us. When we are clear about our passions, strengths, and interests, we can better align our actions with our purpose.

To seek clarity, strip away societal expectations and external pressures. What values and principles resonate deeply with you? What legacy do you wish to leave? Living with intention means aligning your choices with what brings you true contentment and meaning.

REDEFINING WEALTH: A DEEPER FULFILLMENT

We are often conditioned to equate wealth with material gain—money, status, and possessions. However, **true abundance is not found in accumulation but in the depth of our experiences, the love we share, and the inner peace we cultivate.**

As Thich Nhat Hanh wrote in *The Art of Living,* "We run after things that seem very desirable—like money, power, and sex—without realizing the danger in them. We destroy our body and mind chasing after these things, and yet still we continue chasing them. Just as there is a hook hidden in the bait, there is danger hidden in the object of our craving. Once we can see the hook, whatever it is we're craving simply won't be appealing anymore, and we'll be free."

This wisdom highlights the illusion of external success. The constant pursuit of "more" often leads to emptiness rather than fulfillment. When we release the need for validation through wealth or prestige, we create space for what truly enriches life—connection, self-awareness, and peace of mind.

WALK YOUR OWN PATH

One of the greatest barriers to fulfillment is comparison. We are taught to measure ourselves against others, to believe that our worth is reflected in how we stack up to societal ideals. But fulfillment is not a race, nor is it determined by how closely we align with someone else's definition of achievement.

Tend to your own garden, nurture your unique gifts, and allow your journey to unfold organically. **The only person you should compare yourself to is the one you were yesterday.** Growth is deeply personal, and the most rewarding progress comes when we embrace our individuality rather than chase external markers of worth.

IMPACT: THE TRUE MEASURE OF A LIFE WELL LIVED

A meaningful life is not just about personal gain; it is about the difference you make. **The mark you leave on the world is not in titles or possessions but in the lives you touch, the kindness you extend, and the positive change you inspire.**

Consider the ripple effect of your actions—how your words, energy, and choices influence those around you. Whether through small acts of generosity or larger contributions, your purpose gains depth when it uplifts others.

One of the most powerful ways to find purpose is by serving others. Many people discover that their sense of purpose deepens when they contribute to the well-being of others, whether through volunteer work, acts of kindness, or pursuing a career that supports a cause in which they believe.

Helping others provides a sense of meaning that extends beyond personal gain. It allows us to connect with others on a deeper level and reminds us that we are part of something greater than ourselves. Acts of service are often the most fulfilling because they create a sense of purpose that transcends individual needs.

* * *

Finding purpose is an evolving journey—one that requires deep reflection, courage, and openness to change. It is not about chasing an ideal but about uncovering what has been within you all along. When you align your passions, experiences, and values, you create a life rich in meaning.

True fulfillment is not measured by external accomplishments but by inner peace and the impact you have on others. Step into your calling with confidence, embrace the path that is uniquely yours, and trust that you are exactly where you are meant to be.

Self-Care Tips for Discovering Purpose:

- **Reflect on your passions**: Identify what you naturally spend time on, what excites you, and what brings you joy. Your purpose often aligns with what you deeply care about.
- **Learn from struggles**: Your challenges shape your resilience and can guide how you serve others, offering wisdom and empathy.
- **Live with intention**: Strip away societal pressures and focus on values that matter most to you. Align your actions with your passions and strengths.
- **Redefine true wealth**: Shift focus from material wealth to fulfillment through

meaningful experiences, relationships, and inner peace.

- **Walk your own path**: Avoid comparing yourself to others and embrace your unique journey. Growth is personal, and fulfillment comes from nurturing your individuality.
- **Focus on impact**: A meaningful life is measured by the positive influence you have on others. Acts of service and kindness deepen your sense of purpose.

Healing is not about erasing the past but about learning from it, growing through it, and finding beauty in the journey.

Chapter Eleven HEALING

True healing is a journey of integration, where the mind, body, and soul must be nurtured in harmony. It is not a single solution but an ongoing process of self-awareness, growth, and transformation. By embracing wisdom, solitude, mindful living, and deep self-reflection, you create the foundation for inner peace and lasting healing. **While external guidance can be helpful, true healing comes from within.** You take responsibility for your own transformation. Self-realization is the key—understanding that you hold the power to heal yourself. You are empowered to access your own wisdom rather than relying solely on external answers.

THE INTERCONNECTION OF BODY, MIND, AND SOUL

The body, mind, and soul are not separate entities; they are deeply intertwined. Each influences the others in profound ways, and imbalances in one area can create ripple effects throughout the whole system. Physical health can be influenced by emotional stress, and emotional health can be impacted by spiritual disconnect. True healing requires a holistic approach that addresses all aspects of our being.

The Body: The Foundation of Healing

The body is the vessel that carries us through life. When it is unwell, it can affect our energy levels, mood, and overall sense of well-being. Many times, physical ailments are symptoms of deeper emotional or spiritual wounds. Our body speaks to us through illness, pain, and fatigue, signaling when something is out of balance.

Healing the body involves more than just treating physical symptoms; it requires understanding the root causes of disease and addressing them holistically. This might mean incorporating lifestyle changes, improving nutrition, and engaging in physical activities that promote vitality.

The Mind: The Gateway to Healing

The mind is a powerful force. It shapes our perceptions of the world and our responses to it. Negative thought patterns, such as stress, anxiety, and self-doubt, can have a detrimental effect on our mental and physical health. The mind also has the ability to influence the body's immune system, regulate hormones, and manage pain.

Healing the mind involves learning to quiet the inner chatter, shift negative thinking, and cultivate a mindset of peace and positivity. It requires self-awareness and mindfulness, allowing us to observe our thoughts without judgment and to change the patterns that no longer serve us.

The Soul: The Source of True Healing

The soul is the deepest part of who we are. It is our essence, the part of us that connects to something larger than ourselves. Spiritual disconnection can manifest as a feeling of emptiness, a lack of direction, or a sense of being lost. Healing the soul involves reconnecting with our true self and aligning with a sense of purpose and meaning in life.

Spiritual healing is not necessarily about religious practices but about cultivating a sense of inner peace, purpose, and connection to the world around us. It involves nurturing the qualities that are inherent to the soul, such as love, compassion, gratitude, and forgiveness.

SIMPLY BEING: LETTING GO WITH WISDOM

Letting go is an essential part of the healing process. It does not mean avoiding or escaping problems; rather, it is an acceptance of the impermanent nature of all things. Everything changes, and nothing lasts forever. Instead of worrying about what you cannot control, cherish what you have in the present. Protect your heart, uphold your values, and allow life to unfold naturally without clinging or resisting.

Letting go is not about passivity—it is about trust. Trusting that life unfolds in ways beyond our comprehension. It is about setting boundaries while allowing experiences to flow. It is recognizing that attachments, whether to people, success, or even suffering, are fleeting. By accepting this truth, you can engage fully with life without the burden of unnecessary worries.

The practice of simply being invites you to embrace presence. Meditation, breathwork, and moments of stillness teach you to appreciate life as it is, rather than how you think it should be. This shift in perspective fosters gratitude and peace, allowing true healing to occur.

Embrace every lesson along the healing process. Every challenge, every setback, and every experience carry wisdom meant to shape you into a stronger, more enlightened version of yourself. **Healing is not about erasing the past but about learning from it, growing through it, and finding beauty in the journey.** When you surrender to life's flow while honoring your inner wisdom, you open yourself up to deeper self-discovery, resilience, and peace.

A MULTI-FACETED APPROACH TO HEALING

Healing the mind, body, and soul requires a holistic approach that integrates physical, mental, and spiritual well-being. Engaging in movement-based practices such as yoga, tai chi, and qigong supports physical health, while meditation and journaling provide mental clarity. Prioritizing nutritious foods, restful sleep, and an active lifestyle strengthens overall well-being and enhances the body's natural healing abilities. Delving into wisdom traditions like Stoicism and Taoism, Dharma teachings, and mindfulness practices from various cultures fosters resilience and self-awareness and nourishes the soul. Complementary therapies such as sound healing, aromatherapy, and Reiki can further support emotional and energetic healing.

Another powerful method of healing is solitude. Being alone is often misunderstood as loneliness, but true solitude is a powerful tool for self-discovery.

When you create space away from distractions and societal demands, you give yourself the opportunity to listen deeply to your inner voice. Solitude allows you to process emotions, reflect on life, and strengthen your connection with yourself without the noise of the outside world.

Healing is not just about adding new practices but also about removing what no longer serves you. In a world of excess, simplifying your life is an act of self-care. **Identify what is truly important to you, and let go of distractions that drain your time and energy.** By doing so, you create space for clarity, purpose, and peace.

YOU ARE ALREADY WHOLE

Healing begins when you recognize that you are already whole. There is nothing external that can complete you because everything you need is already within. The search for validation, approval, or fulfillment outside yourself is an illusion—one that distracts you from your own inner power. Trust your own truth. Your destiny is in your hands, shaped by your thoughts, choices, and actions. Every answer you seek already exists within you. Have faith in your inner wisdom.

When you stop looking outside yourself for fulfillment, you discover a deep well of peace and strength within. You do not need to chase after success or happiness; rather, you need only to align with your own truth. Understanding your wholeness allows you to engage with the world from a place of abundance rather than lack. You interact with others not from need but from authenticity, connection, and shared experiences.

Embracing your wholeness does not mean you will never struggle or experience pain; it means you will navigate those challenges with wisdom and grace. **True healing is not about erasing difficulties but about cultivating the strength to move through them.** It is about trusting your own journey, knowing that you have everything you need to heal, grow, and thrive.

* * *

Healing is not about fixing yourself; it is about peeling away the layers of conditioning, past wounds, and limiting beliefs that prevent you from seeing your true self. It requires deep self-reflection, an honest assessment of your emotions, and a willingness to face discomfort in order to grow. It is a process of unlearning and rediscovering, of shedding what no longer serves you so that you can return to your essence.

Healing requires patience. It is not a linear path, and setbacks are a natural part of growth. At times, you may feel lost or discouraged, but every step—no matter how small—contributes to your evolution. The process is like tending to a garden; you must nurture yourself with care, allow time for healing, and trust that growth is happening even when you cannot yet see the results. Healing is not a destination but a journey—one that requires courage, patience, and faith in yourself. By integrating these practices into your life, you embark on a path of deep transformation, where mind, body, and soul align in harmony.

Self-Care Tips for Healing:

- **Adopt a holistic approach**: Address the mind, body, and soul in harmony. Each aspect influences the others, so healing requires balancing all areas of well-being.
- **Nurture your body**: Listen to your body, address physical ailments, and support healing with nutrition, movement, and physical self-care.
- **Cultivate mental clarity**: Quiet negative thought patterns through mindfulness and self-awareness, shifting toward peace and positivity.
- **Reconnect with your soul**: Reconnect with your deeper self, cultivating love, compassion, and purpose to heal spiritually.
- **Let go with trust**: Practice acceptance of life's impermanence and trust that life

will unfold as it should, freeing yourself
from unnecessary attachments.

- **Embrace presence**: Engage in
  meditation, breathwork, and stillness to
  foster gratitude and peace, allowing true
  healing to take place.
- **Seek solitude**: Spend time alone to
  reflect, listen to your inner voice, and gain
  self-knowledge away from distractions.
- **Simplify your life**: Remove distractions
  and focus on what truly matters to create
  space for clarity and peace.
- **Recognize your wholeness**:
  Understand that you are already whole
  and that healing is about reconnecting
  with your true self, not fixing something
  that's broken.
- **Be patient with the process**: Healing
  is a journey, not a destination. Embrace
  setbacks as part of the growth process and
  trust that progress happens over time.

By cultivating mindfulness, we open ourselves to the beauty of life in all its forms, learning to live more consciously, with heightened awareness and a deeper sense of inner peace.

Chapter Twelve MINDFULNESS – PATH TO INNER PEACE

Our minds can often feel like wild horses—unpredictable, impulsive, and unruly. Mindfulness, however, offers us the reins to gently guide our thoughts and emotions. Learning to tame this "wild horse" involves mastering the ability to control impulses and find balance in our inner world. It is about accepting the chaos in our minds without allowing it to take control and learning to redirect our attention with patience and care.

Studies show that we are generally less happy when our minds wander, even if the content of our thoughts is pleasant. This highlights the importance of staying present. **When we allow ourselves to drift into the past or future, we miss the beauty and potential of the present moment.** Mindfulness helps us cultivate a deeper sense of satisfaction by anchoring us in the here and now, allowing us to fully experience life as it unfolds.

ACCEPT AND EMBRACE YOUR EMOTIONS, THEN SURRENDER

A crucial aspect of mindfulness is the ability to observe thoughts and emotions without becoming entangled in them. **Rather than reacting impulsively or being swept away by feelings, mindfulness invites you to be a detached observer.** You are not your thoughts or emotions—they are temporary experiences that come and go. When you observe them without identifying with them, you create space between stimulus and response, giving you the power to act with intention rather than react mindlessly.

Mindfulness also encourages embracing emotions rather than suppressing them. Emotions are natural, temporary responses to our experiences. Part of the mindfulness journey is to accept them fully. This doesn't mean acting on every emotion, but rather allowing yourself to feel without resistance. Once you embrace your emotions, you can surrender to the present moment, knowing that all feelings are transient and will pass.

It is important to befriend your mind rather than fight it. Our minds can become chaotic, filled with worry, anxiety, and distractions. Instead of resisting these thoughts, mindfulness encourages us to approach them with compassion and understanding. **The key is not to suppress your thoughts but**

to observe them without judgment. Doing so cultivates a harmonious relationship with your mind, helping you navigate life's challenges with greater peace.

Accept the present moment exactly as it is. We often try to control our circumstances and outcomes, but mindfulness teaches us that control is an illusion. The only thing we truly have is the present moment. It is called the "present" for a reason—it is a gift, and it is all we can ever truly possess. **By letting go of the need for control, we free ourselves from anxiety about the future and regret over the past, allowing us to fully appreciate the now.**

RECOGNIZING YOUR THINKING PATTERNS

A key aspect of mindfulness is becoming aware of your thinking patterns. It's easy to fall into habitual thought loops that reinforce negative beliefs and emotions. However, once you become aware of these patterns, you can begin to change them.

Our minds have a tendency to deceive us, especially when we imagine worst-case scenarios. Catastrophic thinking—where we imagine terrible outcomes that are unlikely to happen—often causes unnecessary stress and anxiety. Buddhist teachings emphasize that human beings frequently view reality through a distorted lens, which leads to unnecessary suffering. This distortion arises from attachments, desires, and fears that cloud our perception of the world. Mindfulness teaches us to recognize when our minds are tricking us into believing things that aren't grounded in reality, helping us see beyond these distortions and experience life as it truly is.

By staying grounded in the present moment, mindfulness helps us break free from these unhelpful patterns and focus on what is truly important. Once you are grounded in the present, try converting negative thoughts into positive ones and making optimism a habit. The way we perceive situations shapes our reality, and by choosing a more constructive perspective, we can cultivate inner peace and resilience. Instead of focusing on what could go wrong, train your mind to see opportunities, lessons, and potential growth in every situation. Over time, this practice rewires the brain to default to positivity rather than fear or doubt.

INCORPORATING MINDFUL PRACTICES INTO YOUR LIFE

Pay attention to the moment. Mindfulness is not confined to a specific time or place—it can be practiced anywhere. Whether walking down the street, sitting at your desk, or waiting in line, you can always choose to focus on the present moment. By paying attention to your breath, the sensations in your body, or the sounds around you, you can anchor yourself in mindfulness throughout your day. Meditation doesn't have to be a formal practice; it can become a way of life where every moment offers an opportunity to be fully present.

Practice mindful self-inquiry. True mindfulness involves turning inward to explore your thoughts and emotions. There is a difference between mindless overthinking and genuine self-reflection. While being lost in thought is the opposite of mindfulness, reflection is a proactive approach to understanding yourself. Mindful self-inquiry allows you to take time to reflect on your experiences, emotions, and behavior patterns. This practice helps you grow, learn, and navigate life with greater wisdom and clarity.

Trust your intuition. Often, we ignore our inner voice in favor of external distractions or the opinions of others. Mindfulness encourages us to tune into our inner wisdom, trusting that it will guide us toward the best path. Your intuition is a powerful tool for decision-making and self-awareness, and when practiced mindfully, it can lead to greater peace and fulfillment.

Explore Mindfulness-Based Stress Reduction (MBSR). One effective way to deepen your mindfulness practice is through structured programs like Mindfulness-Based Stress Reduction (MBSR). Developed by Dr. Jon Kabat-Zinn, MBSR combines mindfulness meditation with body-awareness techniques to help reduce stress and improve well-being. The program teaches participants how to integrate mindfulness into daily life, helping them manage pain, anxiety, and emotional distress more effectively.

Use travel as meditation in motion. Another way to practice mindfulness is through travel. Travel is more than just moving from one place to another—it is an active form of meditation. When you step into unfamiliar surroundings, you are forced to be present. You learn, adapt, and immerse yourself in the moment, making travel a powerful practice of mindfulness. Every journey can be an opportunity for spiritual awakening and deeper self-awareness.

MINDFULNESS REQUIRES SELF-CONTROL AND DISCIPLINE

At its core, mindfulness involves paying attention to the present moment with awareness and without judgment. Nevertheless, this does not happen effortlessly. To cultivate mindfulness, we must develop self-control and discipline. Our minds are naturally restless, often wandering from one thought to the next. **The challenge of mindfulness is learning to return our attention to the present moment again and again, without frustration or judgment.**

Self-control in mindfulness isn't about forcing

yourself into a state of constant attention, but rather about recognizing when our thoughts have drifted and patiently guiding ourselves back to the present. This process requires patience and compassion, not self-criticism. The more you practice, the more naturally you can return your focus to the here and now. Over time, this discipline strengthens your ability to stay grounded in the present moment, reducing the frequency and intensity of distractions.

Discipline in mindfulness also means committing to regular practice. Like any skill, mindfulness requires consistent effort. This doesn't mean practicing for hours every day but rather finding small moments throughout the day to center yourself and bring your awareness back to the present. Whether during a morning routine, a walk, or even mundane tasks like washing dishes, every opportunity to practice strengthens mindfulness until it becomes a way of life.

Through mindfulness, we learn to respond to life's challenges with greater awareness and calm. Instead of reacting impulsively, we choose how to respond with a clear mind. This self-control allows us to approach life with more grace, patience, and resilience, no matter what comes our way.

* * *

Ultimately, mindfulness is a practice that offers profound rewards. It nurtures compassion—both toward ourselves and others—and allows us to navigate life with greater ease, embracing both its joys and challenges with grace. By cultivating mindfulness, we open ourselves to the beauty of life in all its forms, learning to live more consciously, with heightened awareness and a deeper sense of inner peace.

As we continue practicing mindfulness, we come to understand that true peace is not something external to be pursued but rather something we cultivate within. By fostering self-control, embracing our emotions, and remaining anchored in the present, we create a life that is shaped not by external circumstances but by our inner state of being. Mindfulness empowers us to live with true fulfillment, bringing a sense of calm and purpose to every moment.

Self-Care Tips for Practicing Mindfulness:

- **Stay present**: Cultivate mindfulness by anchoring yourself in the present moment. This practice helps reduce stress and enhances your ability to fully experience life.
- **Observe your thoughts and emotions**: Instead of reacting impulsively, practice detachment by observing your emotions and thoughts with curiosity and compassion.

- **Embrace your emotions**: Allow yourself to fully experience emotions without judgment or resistance, understanding that they are temporary and will pass.
- **Recognize thought patterns**: Identify habitual thought patterns, especially negative ones, and shift them to more positive and constructive perspectives.
- **Practice mindfulness throughout the day**: Whether walking, working, or eating, be mindful by focusing on your breath, body sensations, or surroundings.
- **Engage in mindful self-inquiry**: Reflect on your thoughts and behaviors to gain deeper self-awareness and emotional insight, using this as a tool for personal growth.
- **Trust your intuition**: Tune into your inner wisdom. Mindfulness enhances your ability to listen to and trust your instincts.
- **Explore MBSR (Mindfulness-Based Stress Reduction)**: Consider structured mindfulness programs like MBSR to deepen your practice and effectively manage stress and anxiety.
- **Use travel as mindful meditation**: Treat travel as an opportunity for mindfulness by immersing yourself in new

experiences and staying present as you explore unfamiliar places.

- **Cultivate self-control and discipline**: Strengthen mindfulness by gently guiding your attention back to the present whenever it drifts. Regular practice, even in small moments, helps reinforce this skill.

Final Thoughts – To the Child Within Us

few months ago, while on a cruise in the Middle East, I was mesmerized by the vast expanse of the ocean and the gentle rocking of the waves. As I sipped my coffee, my attention was drawn to a toddler sitting in a high chair nearby. He was entirely focused on the small toy in his hand, turning it, examining it, delighting in its simple presence. Then, as toddlers do, he accidentally dropped it. Without hesitation or frustration, he simply reached for another toy and began playing with it, just as engaged and curious as before. There was no mourning of the lost toy, no distraction from the present moment—just a pure, effortless embrace of what was in front of him.

That moment stuck with me.

Children have an extraordinary ability to be present in the moment, something many of us lose as we grow older. We become consumed by past mistakes or anxious about the future, allowing stress and doubt to cloud our minds. But children? They live in the now. They feel their emotions fully, express them honestly, and then move forward without suppressing or carrying unnecessary burdens.

Watching that little boy made me reflect on all the invaluable lessons children unknowingly teach us. They remind us to be fearless—to step into the unknown with excitement rather than apprehension. They don't overthink things; they don't complicate matters with endless "what-ifs." They experience joy in the smallest things—a bubble floating in the air, the sound of laughter, the warmth of the sun. They dream without limits, without societal constraints telling them what is or isn't possible.

As adults, we often seek understanding and progress, but in doing so, we sometimes forget that these are not just about accumulating knowledge. It's also about remembering the things we once knew as children: how to savor life's simple pleasures, how to be honest with our feelings, and how to approach life with a heart wide open.

This is why I chose to release this book on June 1st, International Children's Day—not just to celebrate children, but to remind us to reconnect with the child within. To live fearlessly. To dream without limits. To be free from worry. To live in the present moment and delight in life's simplest joys.

May we never forget to play. May we never stop being curious. May we always carry the spirit of childhood within us—for it is in that spirit that we find the courage to grow.